Hall of Mirrors

by Phil Preece

Illustrated by David Cuzik

Contents

Chapter 1

Carrie sat on a bench looking out over the ocean.

It was hot and sunny up here on the seafront. Crowds of holidaymakers were walking along enjoying themselves, wearing shorts and eating ice creams.

Down on the beach people sat in deckchairs. Some were playing ball games on the sand. Children splashed in the sea, screaming at the waves.

But Carrie was miserable. She was wishing she was at home.

She'd left Mum and Dad down there on the beach. It was too boring stopping with them.

Carrie used to love the seaside when she was a little girl. But not now. She wanted to be with the friends she'd left back home.

She'd tried smiling at a group of girls as they went by. They just stared at her, and then walked on. After that she didn't bother. She felt too embarrassed to try.

What was the point of coming on holiday when it was no fun?

Carrie decided she might as well go for a walk.

As she wandered along she felt more and more depressed.

It was late afternoon now. People had already started heading for home.

Then she saw it up ahead.

The old pier.

It stuck out into the ocean, rusty and falling apart, like a row of rotting teeth. It looked as if it might fall down at any time.

Carrie walked up to the entrance. There was an old metal turnstile. It was broken, and she pushed through. No need to pay.

Ahead of her she saw a sign – "Amusement Arcade". The paint was peeling off it. Better than nothing, she supposed. Might as well give it a try. She set off towards the arcade along the bare planks of the pier.

The shabby door didn't look very inviting. Pushing it open cautiously, she crept in. It was dark inside after the sunlight. Old-fashioned slot machines lurked silently in the gloom. The place seemed to be deserted. Carrie shivered. This place was giving her the creeps.

Back in the light she let the door swing shut. That was no good.

Ahead she saw another sign. "Hall of Mirrors" it said.

Carrie went up the few steps to the entrance. There was no one to take her money here either. I'll just look inside, she thought.

She stepped into the dark interior. There in front of her was a mirror – but one with a difference. It stretched her reflection out until she was long and thin. She moved, and her head was two feet tall. Carrie started to smile. So far this was the best thing that had happened all day.

She moved on to the next mirror. This one squashed her down until she was as wide as a bus but only knee high. This was great. She was enjoying herself now.

Each of the mirrors did something different. One of them bent in the middle, making her look fat and thin at the same time. Carrie ran from one to the other, laughing at all the strange shapes she was making. By the time she came to the last one she was nearly doubled up with laughter.

And then suddenly she noticed something that froze her laugh in her throat. It was a face next to hers in the mirror. It was pale as a ghost, and its reflection seemed to be floating in the glass.

Carrie gasped. Her heart seemed to stop beating.

Then she took a deep breath and straightened herself up. Slowly she turned to see what was behind her.

It was a young man. He was all dressed in black, and his handsome face was as pale as it had seemed in the mirror.

"I'm sorry," he said. "Did I scare you?"

Carrie's mouth had gone dry.

"Yes," she said. "I mean no."

"You seemed to be enjoying yourself. Don't let me stop you."

Then he smiled. Carrie felt her heart start beating again. He was real flesh and blood after all. She smiled back.

"Do you work here?" Carrie asked. "I – I haven't paid."

The young man laughed.

"Pay next time," he said.

His eyes were dark, and he seemed to be looking right into her.

"What's your name?"

"Carrie."

"I'm Jim," he said. As he spoke he was moving away from her, and she saw his reflection distorted a hundred times in the mirrors that stood all around.

"See you again," he said.

Then he was gone.

Carrie stared after him. She let out a huge sigh. He was gorgeous. And he'd said he'd like to see her again.

Suddenly things were looking up. She'd found a friend. Maybe this holiday wasn't going to be so bad after all.

Just then she noticed something odd. The boy had left a trail of footprints. Wet footprints.

That's strange, thought Carrie, stepping out into the sunlight.

The day was perfectly dry.

Chapter 2

Carrie was back at the hotel in time for the evening meal.

Two or three other families were in the dining room tonight.

"Ah," said Dad, smacking his lips. "Fish and chips. Just the thing at the seaside."

The landlady, Mrs Matthews, was waiting on the tables. She was chatting away all the time like she usually did.

"The weather's keeping nice for you, anyway," she was saying to a young couple in the corner.

Their two little boys were busy kicking each other under the table.

Carrie's mother looked across at her husband.

"I'm glad to see our Carrie's looking a bit happier," she said in a quiet voice.

Carrie didn't notice. She was staring dreamily out of the window.

"Eh, come on, don't let them chips go cold," said her dad.

Carrie came back out of her trance.

"Oh," she said. "No." She started to eat them mechanically. Then suddenly she realized how hungry she was and started to wolf them down.

"Our Carrie's had a lovely time today on your pier," said her dad to Mrs Matthews in a loud voice.

"Oh?" said the landlady, pausing for a minute. "That old thing? Ought to be pulled down if you ask me."

The two lads were fighting now over the ketchup. One of them had the top off. With a jerk he spilt it all over the cloth.

"She's lucky she could get on that pier at all. Nearly washed away it did, a few years ago."

Mrs Matthews put her tray down to rest it while she talked.

"What happened?" asked Carrie.

"Well. It was a freak storm. Came up out of nowhere. Just about this time of year it was."

By now the two lads had stopped fighting and were listening. Their mouths hung open wide.

"Terrible it was. It came at the end of a very hot day. Lightning, thunder, the lot. And wind – a terrible wind came up out of the sea. Nobody had ever seen anything like it. Then at the

height of the storm there was this giant wave.
A storm surge I think they call it. It covered the
pier. Nearly washed the whole thing away."

Everyone in the room had gone quiet.
Even Dad had stopped eating. He sat with his
fork halfway up to his mouth.

Mrs Matthews went on almost as if she
was talking to herself.

"A young lad who worked there in the amusement arcade was drowned. A lovely young lad. He was swept away by the wave. His body was never found."

There was complete silence in the room. Then suddenly the boys' mother noticed what they'd been up to.

"Oh you little devils!" she said. "Look what you've done to that nice clean cloth! Whatever will Mrs Matthews think of us?"

"Never mind," said Mrs Matthews. "No harm done. Worse things happen at sea."

Carrie was staring out of the window again. She was wondering what the boy had been like. The one who'd been drowned in the storm.

⁂

Carrie was back on the pier again the next afternoon. She told herself it was because she had nothing better to do. But secretly she was hoping to bump into Jim again.

There were a few people on the pier when she got there, but not many. It was swelteringly hot.

She hung around for ages but couldn't see Jim anywhere.

She looked in the Amusement Arcade, and in the Hall of Mirrors. She'd thought he worked there, but now she wasn't so sure. Maybe it was his day off.

At last it was nearly evening. From the pier Carrie could see everyone leaving the beach.

She leaned against the railing staring out to sea. Behind her the sun was just beginning to set. The whole sky seemed to be on fire.

A shadow fell across the rail next to her. As she turned, for a second the blazing sun dazzled her eyes. A dark shape was silhouetted against the sunset. It seemed to tower over her, black against the light. Its huge distorted shadow stretched towards her as if it would like to swallow her up.

She took a step back against the railing. Then in a moment the shape seemed to shrink and she recognized who it was.

"Oh, Jim!" She sighed with relief. "For a minute I thought – I mean – you startled me. Oh, you did make me jump!" She gave a shaky little laugh.

Without a word he took her by the hand, and together they walked along the deserted pier. The sun was falling into the ocean in a blaze of light. Jim seemed distracted, looking far out over the sea. When Carrie tried to talk to him he hardly seemed to hear.

Still, it was lovely walking there together in the sunset. Just being with him made her feel really great.

When it was time to go, Jim held her tightly by the arms for a moment. His dark eyes looked deep into hers.

Carrie reached up and touched his hair before she turned to leave him. It was wet, as if he'd been swimming in the sea.

Chapter 3

"I'm worried," said Carrie's mum.

She and her husband were sitting side by side in deckchairs on the beach.

"What about, love?" Dad was dozing off in the sunshine.

"She's spending too much time on that pier. I don't like it. I don't know what she does up there. She's there nearly all day long."

"Well what do you want me to do?" he asked.

"Try to stop her. Get her to spend some time with us for a change."

"Well," said Dad. "I'll try."

That night he was as good as his word. They were in the hotel sitting room after dinner.

"What about a picnic?" he asked. "Eh, love?"

"What do you mean?" asked Carrie.

"A picnic with us on the beach. Tomorrow. Just like we used to have."

"No thanks," said Carrie. "I'm busy."

"Busy with what?" asked her mother.

"Just busy," said Carrie. She turned to look out of the window. She looked lost in her own little world.

Just then Michael, the landlady's son, came into the sitting room.

He looked over in Carrie's direction.

"Anybody fancy coming out for a walk?" he asked cheerfully. "Me and some of my friends are going up to the fair."

"Go on, Carrie," said her mother. "She'll go with you, Michael. Won't you love?"

"No thanks," said Carrie. She could see a group of boys and girls waiting for Michael outside. They were all about her own age. But all she wanted to do was stay and think about Jim.

"I'm still worried," said her mum after Carrie had gone to bed. "I don't like this. She's really changed. She doesn't seem to want to do anything anymore. It's like she's under a spell."

"She'll be all right," said her dad. "She's just going through a phase. They all do. It'll wear off."

"I'm not so sure," said her mother. Absent-mindedly she fingered the little gold cross she wore on a chain round her neck. "I'm not so sure," she repeated thoughtfully to herself.

It was true. Carrie was spending all her time on the pier. She'd started going there every day straight after breakfast. Then she hung around all day hoping to get a glimpse of Jim.

Some days he was already there waiting for her. Then they walked along the pier together hand in hand, laughing at everything and nothing. Jim seemed interested in everything Carrie said, even the silly little things. Sometimes as they walked he put his arm around her. Carrie smiled at the memory. Jim was special. He was someone who really cared.

Other times he failed to turn up until late in the afternoon. Sometimes she'd almost given up hope of him coming. But he always showed up in the end.

He was late today. Carrie had waited and waited, but still he hadn't come. She didn't mind. She was used to it. She knew he wouldn't let her down.

But when six o'clock came she began to wonder if he really was coming. It was nearly time to go back for the evening meal, but still she hung on. He might come even now.

Finally she had no choice but to leave.

Carrie trailed down the pier towards the exit feeling miserable. Where was he? Perhaps something had happened to him. She felt she'd die if she couldn't see him. Reluctantly she set off back to the hotel.

In the dining room she sat in silence staring down at the table.

"You've hardly touched your tea," her dad said.

"I can't eat it."

Her mum and dad exchanged glances.

"Come on love. For me," said her dad.

"I can't," she said.

She got up.

"I've got to go now."

"But you can't," said her mother.

"I can," said Carrie. "I must. I've got to."
She ran out of the room.

Michael was in the hall on his way to the kitchen. Carrie pushed past without even seeing him.

He just caught a glimpse of her expression. Her eyes were staring. She looked like someone possessed.

Carrie ran out of the house before anyone could stop her. She couldn't get the picture of Jim out of her mind. Nothing else but him mattered.

She had to see him again.

Chapter 4

It was almost dark by the time Carrie got
back to the pier. Only a last trace of daylight
was left in the sky.

A string of coloured lights burnt above
the entrance. Some of the bulbs were missing.
It made Carrie think of a grin with gaps in its
teeth.

She slipped easily onto the pier through the broken turnstile.

Everything felt strange. She'd never been here on her own in the evening before. The pier looked different with the stalls and amusements all lit up. Dark shadows filled the spaces in between.

Her feet seemed to know the way without her having to tell them.

Soon she was standing outside the Hall of Mirrors. This was where she had first seen Jim. Perhaps he'd be here tonight when she wanted him so much.

A dim light was on in the ticket office. Carrie felt in her pocket. Then in panic she turned it inside out. With a shock she realized she had run out without bringing any money.

How on earth was she going to get inside?

She slipped into the shadows at the side of the building. She needed time to think.

It was absolutely quiet here. No one else seemed to be about. In the silence Carrie could hear the dark waves under her feet lapping against the pier.

Just then a man came out of the ticket office. He went round the side of the building and disappeared.

Quick! This was her only chance. In a flash she dashed out of the shadows and ran up the steps.

Inside the Hall of Mirrors it was dark. The lights hadn't been switched on yet. At first she couldn't see anything. Then gradually she caught the faint gleam of mirrors stretching away into the distance.

All around she saw dim crooked reflections of herself. In one, her bloated shape spread out until it filled the whole glass.

In another she was painfully thin. Her snake-like body was stretched out into a sinister narrow shape.

Tonight the reflections didn't seem funny. They were ugly and disturbing. She moved on hastily. If only she could find Jim.

Ahead of her was one last shadowy mirror. Carrie felt its darkness drawing her towards it. She gazed into it as if it held the answer to all her questions. Her head swirled. She felt as if she were drowning in its depths.

Carrie thought she could see a faint light deep inside it. A door seemed to open somewhere far away.

Then as she watched a distant figure appeared walking towards her. Slowly it drew nearer until it faced her from the other side of the glass.

Carrie blinked.

The shadow held out a hand for her to take it.

She felt her flesh prickle. Was she dreaming? She shook her head to try to clear it.

Then from behind she felt the faint touch of a hand on her shoulder.

She spun round with a horrible jolt. A handsome face was laughing into her own.

"Jim," she said. She could feel her heart pounding. Why, she wondered? There was nothing to be afraid of. What she had seen was only a trick of the light.

"Time to go," said Jim, taking her by the hand. Carrie let him lead her.

Outside a cool wind was blowing off the sea. Night had fallen. In the sky the moon was almost full. White and cold it sailed through the rushing clouds.

Hand in hand they walked along the pier together in the brilliant moonlight. Carrie felt as if she were floating. She was happier than she had ever been before.

At the farthest end of the pier they halted. The moonlight made a glittering track across the ocean.

"Carrie."

Jim's shining eyes reflected the white moon.

"I wish we could be together always."

He held her close to him. Then he bent his head to kiss her. At that moment the moon went behind a cloud.

Was it only her imagination? His lips felt cold, cold as the kiss of death.

His voice seemed to come from very far away.

"Will you make me a promise?" he asked. "Meet me here tomorrow night. There's something I have to tell you."

Carrie nodded slowly. She would do anything for him.

Already it was time for them to part. For a last moment Jim's fingers touched her hand. Then he was gone.

Sadly she stared after him as he vanished into the night.

Where he had been standing lay something dark and twisted. She stooped to touch it.

It was a wreath of seaweed, sandy and wet as if fresh from the sea.

At breakfast the next morning there was definitely an atmosphere.

Mum and Dad hadn't said anything, but Carrie could tell she was in disgrace.

After breakfast Dad went out to buy a paper. Mum went upstairs to write postcards in her room.

Carrie was left alone in the dining room. Mrs Matthews came in and started clearing the tables.

"You know that storm you said nearly wrecked the pier?" Carrie felt shy at hearing herself ask the question.

Mrs Matthews paused in what she was doing. "Yes," she said, after a moment.

"Did you ever know the name of that boy? The one who was drowned?"

Mrs Matthews looked hard at Carrie before she gave her answer.

"Yes," she said. "I did. His name was Jim McGregor."

Carrie shivered. She felt as if someone had just walked over her grave.

Chapter 5

The rest of the day seemed to last forever. For some reason Mum and Dad didn't seem to want to let her out of their sight.

They insisted on going out for a bus ride all along the seafront – in the opposite direction to the pier.

Later they looked at shops, bought postcards, stopped and had a drink in a pub, and went for a walk in the park.

But all the time Carrie could only think about one thing. She couldn't wait for the day to end, and the night to come. Then she would be alone again with Jim.

It was the same after they got back to the hotel.

Mum had arranged with Mrs Matthews for them to have an early meal. As a treat Dad had got tickets for them to see a show. The star was Dad's favourite comedian, and there were lots of other acts as well.

Somehow Carrie didn't seem to be able to get out of it. They set out for the theatre early. Mum said there was no point in them being late.

All through the performance Carrie found her mind wandering. The image of the pier kept coming before her, with the moon and the dark water lapping underneath. Jim was nowhere to be seen. She felt she must go there and look for him. It was a surprise when the lights went on and Dad was asking her if she'd like an ice cream.

The second half of the show starred Dad's comedian. He must have been good, because all the people around her were laughing their heads off.

But Carrie couldn't wait for the performance to end. And when it did, Mum and Dad were very firm about going straight back to the hotel. It was late, they said. They could all do with a good night's sleep.

It was a hot night, and when she got into bed Carrie just couldn't rest. Jim would be waiting. Mum and Dad hadn't given her a single chance to get away to the pier all day.

In a way she was almost glad. She was worn out with thinking about it.

The room seemed to be getting hotter. Carrie got up and opened the window. A tiny breeze stirred the curtains. A breath of hot air came into the room.

She looked down at the deserted street. Then without another thought she put on her clothes. Silently opening her door she crept downstairs. The front door was bolted and it took what seemed like hours to ease it open. But at last she was on the other side of it, out in the night.

The hot streets were deserted. Carrie had never been out in the town this late before.

She hurried, always drawing nearer and
nearer to the pier. Soon her heart was
pounding in her chest.

At last she saw the pier ahead of her. It was all in darkness. Carrie halted. It was closed. Did she dare to go on the pier so late alone?

She went up to the old turnstile. It was padlocked, but in a moment she had climbed over it. As she touched it, the rusted metal grated. The noise sounded loud as a scream in the quiet night.

Next minute she was on the darkened pier. She stood still and listened. The pier was still too, as if it were waiting. The tide was up. Only the sound of the waves disturbed the silence.

Suddenly she felt a fool. Surely Jim would have given up waiting for her long ago? But something beyond herself made her go on.

As she stepped forward her footfalls seemed to echo. She picked her way carefully in the darkness. At last she came to the very end of the pier.

Even here the heat was suffocating. Carrie could hear the restless waves slapping against the pier's rusted iron girders.

Maybe he would still come, thought Carrie. She settled down to wait. If he did she would be here for him, like always.

The sky above was clear. Carrie watched the full moon rise out of the sea. Swiftly it climbed high into the sky. Its bright rays cast hard shadows behind everything as she waited on.

And then when she was almost dozing she heard running footsteps. Suddenly Jim was there. He was out of breath, as if he had run a very long way.

He stood before Carrie, the moon reflected in his eyes.

"I have to go away," he said.

"No," said Carrie. She began to cry. "Let me come with you."

The night was still. The air was stifling. Carrie looked out over the sea. There on the horizon was a low bank of cloud that had not been there before.

"No," said Jim. "I have to go alone."

From the distance came a low rumble of thunder. A wind had sprung up. Carrie's hair whipped against her face.

Then in an instant Jim seemed to change his mind. Carrie saw a gleam in his eyes that may only have been the moonlight.

They were standing near the pier's railing. Jim gripped Carrie by the arms. His grip was so fierce it hurt.

"All right," he said. "You can come with me."

The storm had crept up on them unawares. Suddenly there was a brilliant flash of lightning and a disastrous crash of thunder. A wild gale was blowing. Rain in great sheets had begun to fall. Thunder crashed again and lightning struck the surface of the sea all around them. Now the waves had become huge, thudding against the pier.

The pier itself began to shake under them.

Through the shrieking of the wind Carrie tried to think. In the lurid glare of the lightning Jim's head was thrown back. For one awful moment she saw his face fixed in a terrible grin.

All at once Carrie realized what it was she had tried to ignore. As the lightning flashed again he turned to look at her. Her heart grew cold in her body.

She saw Jim now for what he really was. A demon, the ghost of a drowned boy. He had come back from the sea to take her down to hell.

Chapter 6

Carrie felt one moment of pure terror.

She screamed. Then in a frenzy she fought to wrench herself free.

The dead hands only tightened their bony grip.

Slowly, relentlessly she felt herself being drawn towards the railing.

The storm was rising to its height. She seemed to be in its very centre. Electricity crackled all around. Blue lightning snaked along the railings. The sea rose in a boiling mass. Blinding forks of white flame struck its seething surface again and again.

Carrie struggled wildly. She finally realized what the ghost intended. He had come to claim her. Now he was going to drown her in the sea. That way she would be with him for ever.

She looked up. This was the boy she'd begged to take her away with him. But the handsome Jim had gone. In his place was a skull with empty holes for eyes. The lips she had kissed had rotted long ago. The teeth gleamed like tombstones in a revolting grin.

She opened her mouth to scream again. This time no sound came out.

Carrie knew she had only one choice now. She must escape.

Slowly, desperately, one by one she tried to peel the skeleton fingers away from her wrists. They clung ever tighter with an inhuman strength.

"I will do it," she gasped through clenched teeth.

She wanted to live. Nothing was going to stop her.

She tried again. This time, slowly, agonisingly she felt her hands slide free.

There was no time to lose. Slipping and sliding on the wet boards she ran for all she was worth.

"Help me," she whispered. "Help me."

Her only answer was the wind howling around her. The wailing of a thousand dead voices seemed to be in it.

Time was standing still like in a nightmare. Her feet felt clogged as if by quicksand. She looked back. The ghostly skeleton had vanished. But now invisible fingers clutched and tugged at her, pulling her ever nearer to the water's edge.

"You can't have me!" she shouted. "Let me go!"

The voices laughed mockingly. Yet ever so slightly the clutching hands seemed to slacken their grip.

Ahead she could see the entrance to the pier. Step by step she pushed her aching body forward.

Demon voices were calling to her out of the storm. "Stay with us. Stay!"

"No!" screamed Carrie. "No! You'll never have me!"

The clutching hands fell away. Carrie felt strength returning to her body. Her feet seemed lighter. She could move more freely. Next minute she was running.

Now the entrance was only just ahead of her. With a last desperate burst of energy she threw herself across the turnstile. Her feet touched the pavement. She was back on the safety of dry land.

At once an unearthly wail rose high above the sound of thunder. A thousand dead voices sobbed for the loss of their prey.

Carrie stood gasping and trembling with tiredness. Her clothes were wet through.

From far out at sea there was a dull roar. Carrie raised her throbbing head. Out on the horizon a giant wave had risen. She had one sickening glimpse of it through the curtain of rain. There was no time to think. The storm surge was sweeping in.

Was this the way it had happened once before?

With the last ounce of strength that was in her she fled for her life. Across the seafront she ran. Then up the steep grassy bank that sheltered the town from the sea's fury. Would it be high enough to save her? Madly she clawed her way up it in desperation.

Carrie had hardly reached the top before the wave hit. Turning, she saw it rear up like a terrible wall. Then with a roar it broke. With a groan the old pier vanished under it. The tide rose high over the seafront. Spray drenched Carrie even where she stood. Then the sea rolled on. Its surface surged and swelled like melted glass.

The waves pulled backwards with a harsh rattle of stones. The pier had gone along with everything on it. It had all been washed away and completely destroyed.

Already people were coming out in ones and twos to look at the damage. Soon there were dozens staring at where the pier had been wrenched like a rotten tooth from its socket.

The storm was moving away. The last rolls of thunder were dying out over the sea.

Now there were people coming towards her. Someone put a coat round Carrie's shoulders. She recognized Michael and some of his friends. Together they stood and watched in silence as the last of the rain washed over them.

The sea was calmer now. The rain had stopped.

The moon came out and looked down at them once again.

At last they set off together for home through the deserted streets. Carrie walked a little way ahead. Michael and his friends followed talking in low voices. The moon shone in puddles that were already drying on the pavement.

Carrie had a lot to think about as she walked. The ghost had gone for ever, she knew. But she had saved herself only just in time.

At the hotel Mum and Dad were waiting for her on the doorstep.

"Welcome back, love," said her dad.

Her mum didn't say anything. She just reached out and took Carrie in her arms.

Carrie gave a great sigh.

"Well," she said. "I'm home."

It felt good to be alive.